Home Life in Ancient Rome

Daniel C. Gedacht

ROSEN CLASSROOM
PRIMARYSOURCE
Rosen Classroom Books & Materials

For Andrew and Cicely

Published in 2004 by The Rosen Publishing Group, Inc.
29 East 21st Street, New York, NY 10010

First Edition

Editor: Rachel O'Connor
Book Design: Michael J. Caroleo
Photo Researcher: Adriana Skura

Photo Credits: Cover © Giraudon/Art Resource, NY; cover (inset) © Reunion des Musées Nationaux/Art Resource, NY; pp. 4, 11 (bottom) The Art Archive/Museo della Civilta Romana Rome/Dagli Orti; pp. 7, 16 The Art Archive/Musée Luxembourgeois Arlon Belgium/Dagli Orti; pp. 8 (top), 12 The Granger Collection, New York; p. 8 (bottom) The Art Archive/Dagli Orti; p. 11 (top) The Art Archive/Musée du Louvre Paris/Dagli Orti; p. 12 © Erich Lessing/Art Resource, NY; p. 15 © SEF/Art Resource, NY; p. 19 (top) The Art Archive/Archeological Museum Naples/Dagli Orti; p. 19 (bottom) © Chwatsky/Art Resource, NY.

Gedacht, Daniel C.
Home life in ancient Rome / Daniel C. Gedacht.— 1st ed.
    p. cm.— (Primary sources of ancient civilizations. Rome)
Includes bibliographical references and index.
  ISBN 0-8239-6778-6 (library binding)—ISBN 0-8239-8945-3 (pbk.)
1. Rome—Social life and customs—Juvenile literature. 2. Family—Rome—Juvenile literature. I. Title. II. Series.
  DG90 .G44 2004
  937—dc21

                                                                                    2003002329

Manufactured in the United States of America

Contents

The Roman Family

The center of ancient Roman life was the family. Family was viewed as the building block of society. The father, called the paterfamilias, was the head of the family. He ruled with absolute authority. The Romans were encouraged to have many children because Rome needed people to serve in the army. The army helped keep Rome powerful. From the fifth century B.C., Romans fought in many wars.

During the rule of Augustus, from 27 B.C. to A.D. 14, the government gave privileges such as extra grain and reduced taxes to families with many children. Rome needed children who would grow up to become soldiers, scholars, and merchants.

◀ *Because family was so important to ancient Romans, wealthy Romans often had images of their family members carved into the family tomb.*

Marriage

In both rich and poor families, the parents usually arranged marriages for their children. Around the first century B.C., patrician, or upper-class, families began to pay cash dowries to the husband's family when their daughters married. Fathers could legally promise their children for marriage when the children turned seven years old. Girls could marry when they were 12, and boys when they were 14. On her wedding day, the bride wore an orange veil. A large group of family and friends walked with the new bride to her new home where her husband waited. After they blessed the door with olive oil, the husband carried his new wife into their home.

This third-century A.D. sculpture shows a young married couple. In ancient Rome, the main reason for a couple to marry was to have children. ▶

8

The Role of Women

The women in Rome had little power and few legal rights. They lived at the mercy of their fathers, their husbands, or their husbands' fathers. Romans believed that the main purpose of patrician women was to have children. The women spent their days either with their children or visiting friends. Plebeian, or lower-class, women and slave women were also urged to have children. Apart from raising a family, they also had much more to do. The poorer women had to do all the housework, prepare meals, work in the fields sometimes, and make the family's clothing. They also taught their daughters the skills they would need when they were sent off to another family for marriage.

A woman is bathing a young child in this picture made from small pieces of stone or tile. Inset: This is what a Roman kitchen might have looked like in the first century A.D.

Roman Children

Roman children enjoyed games such as tag and hide-and-seek. Many had pet dogs. The girls played with dolls made from clay or wax, and boys played games with blocks made from ivory. Plebeian boys learned practical skills from their fathers, such as how to farm or ride horses. At age seven, some boys and girls went to school to study reading, writing, and mathematics. Most children finished their basic schooling before their teens. When boys finished school, they worked as farmers, craftsmen, or soldiers. Girls learned from their mothers how to cook, sew, and spin cloth. Wealthier boys were able to continue studying. They learned subjects such as law and history.

Top: *Here Roman boys are playing a game together.*
Bottom: *Roman schoolchildren might have used tablets and bronze* ▶
inkwells such as these, which belonged to the scholar Theodoros.

(11)

(12)

Slaves

From the beginning of Roman history, Romans owned slaves. Slaves often lived in the family home. In early Rome, slaves were usually treated well, and many were freed when their masters died. In the third century B.C., however, things changed. Rome expanded its territory by conquering areas of Africa, northern Europe, and the Middle East. The military captured and enslaved many people from these places. These foreign slaves were often treated badly, and they revolted. For example, in 73 B.C., a deserter named Spartacus led a group of about 120,000 slaves against Roman forces.

◀ *Slaves and servants completed many tasks for their masters, including pouring wine for meals and banquets, as these servants are doing here.* Bottom: *Many people died during the slave revolt led by Spartacus.*

Roman Homes

There was limited space in the city of Rome, which made housing expensive. Most plebeian families could not afford private homes. They lived in small one- or two-room apartments in large buildings made of wood, cement, and brick. These buildings were so large they filled an entire city block. They were called *insulae*, or islands. Wealthy families could afford to build grand houses in the city. These homes had marble floors and columns, many paintings and murals, and gold and silver decorations. The rich also had large farm estates in the country. These were usually built around a central courtyard or a sitting room, called an atrium.

This courtyard forms an open-air dining room for a Roman home. On one of the walls is a painting of the gods Neptune and Amphitrite. ▶

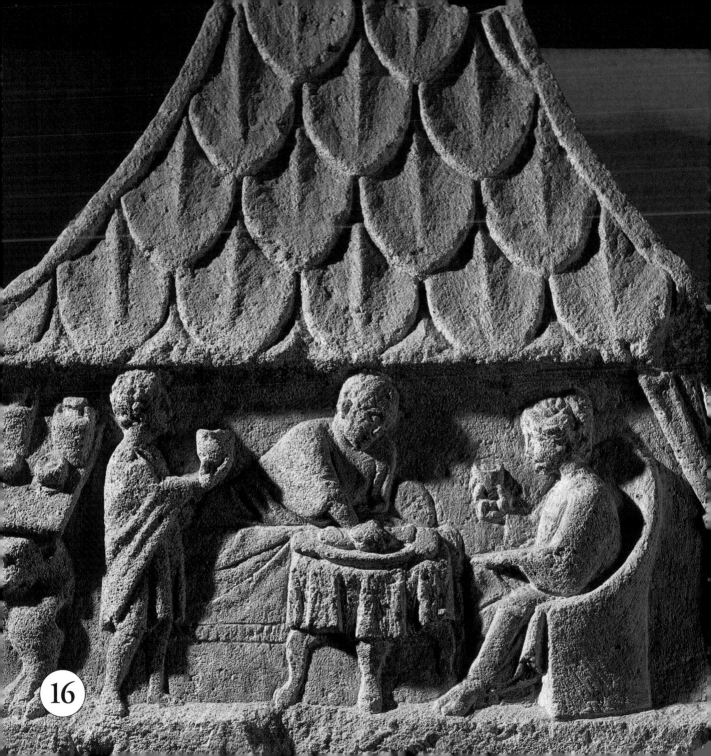

What the Romans Ate

Most Romans ate breakfast at sunrise and then went to work or study. They returned home for a large dinner, called *cena*, at around two o'clock in the afternoon. After this they returned to work. Patricians spent time at the public baths.

In the countryside people grew most of their food, but in the city people shopped at large open markets such as the Roman Forum. Most Romans ate mainly bread, barley, fruit, olives, and fish. Some families owned a cow or chickens and so they could have milk, cheese, and eggs. The wealthier Romans often held large dinner parties and feasted on mushrooms, oysters, sardines, fish, and meats such as wild boar and ostrich.

◀ *In this sculpture from the second century A.D., a Roman family enjoys a meal together in their home.*

Sports and Entertainment

In their free time, the ancient Romans enjoyed watching events that exhibited strength and power. They watched men race chariots around oval tracks. They also attended gladiator matches, in which men fought each other to the death. Tigers, lions, and panthers were sometimes let loose in an arena to hunt and be hunted by gladiators.

Romans also took part in more relaxing activities. During the second century B.C., large baths, called *thermae*, became popular. At first only men could go. By the end of the first century B.C., though, there were separate chambers for men and women. The baths were comfortable places to exercise and relax.

These ancient Roman baths are located in Bath, England, once part of the Roman Empire. Inset: Gladiators wore helmets made from bronze. ▶

Roman Clothes

The mark of Roman citizenship was the toga, a large sheet wrapped around the body. Only citizens could wear togas. Children wore togas that had a purple stripe on the border, which showed they were not yet full citizens. When they became adults, at around age 15, they would wear plain togas. Patricians often wore colored clothes. Important officials such as emperors, senators, and consuls had purple bands and gold threads around the edges of their togas. Married women wore long tunics called *stolas* that reached their ankles. In public, women usually covered their heads with scarves. Non-citizens wore woolen pants and coarse shirts.

◄ *A philosopher is shown in this mosaic, or picture made from small pieces of stone or tile, wearing a toga in the style of male citizens.*

A Sense of Community

The Romans followed *pietas*, which was the belief that every person should be responsible and loyal to his or her family and to the gods of Rome. The paterfamilias was responsible for his family, and the family had responsibilities to other families, the government, and the gods. In the same way, the government was responsible for making sure that the people in Rome had enough food and were safe from enemies. The Romans also believed that it was important for people to have faith, called *fides*, in one another. To the ancient Romans, a promise was like a signed contract. To break one's word was unacceptable not only to the family, but also to society as a whole. For Romans, all of Rome was a sort of family.

Glossary

arena (uh-REE-nuh) A fenced or walled-in space that is used for events.

banquets (BAN-kwets) Large meals eaten in honor of a holiday or special event.

chariots (CHAR-ee-uts) Two-wheeled battle cars pulled by horses.

craftsmen (KRAFTS-men) Workmen who practice a certain trade.

deserter (dih-ZURT-er) Someone who runs away while serving with an army.

dowries (DOW-reez) The money or property that a woman brings to her husband when they get married.

expanded (ek-SPAND-ed) Spread out, or grew larger.

foreign (FOR-in) Outside one's own country.

gladiators (GLA-dee-ay-turs) People who fought against other men or animals to the death.

legal (LEE-gul) Allowed by the law.

loyal (LOY-ul) Faithful to a person or an idea.

murals (MYUR-ulz) Pictures painted on a wall that usually cover most of the wall.

philosopher (fih-LAH-suh-fer) A person who tries to discover and to understand the basic nature of knowledge.

privileges (PRIV-lij-ez) Special rights or favors.

revolted (rih-VOLT-ed) Fought or rebelled.

scholars (SKAH-lerz) People who have gone to school and who have much knowledge.

tomb (TOOM) A grave.

tunics (TOO-niks) Large, loose shirts.

Index

Primary Sources

Cover. A family banquet. Roman relief. Museo della Civilta Romana. Third century A.D. **Inset.** Jug decorated with winged genius offering a drink to a griffin. **Page 4.** Polygonal stele of Fuficia family. Museo della Civilta Romana. First century A.D. **Page 7.** Young married couple. Third-century A.D. relief. **Page 8. Top.** Washing a child. Mosaic from the House of Theseus, Paphos, Cyprus. Third century A.D. **Page 11. Top.** Children playing with nuts. Relief from Ostia, Italy. Second century A.D. Museo della Civilta Romana. **Page 12. Top.** Two servants decanting wine. Tomb relief. Second to third centuries A.D. Rheinisches Landesmuseum. **Page 15.** Courtyard forming an open-air dining room. One wall is decorated with a mosaic representing Neptune and Amphitrite. Circa first century A.D. **Page 16.** Meal inside a house. Second-century A.D. relief. Musée Luxembourgeois, Belgium. **Page 19. Inset.** Gladiator's helmet from Pompeii, Italy. Bronze. First century A.D. Archaeologica Museum, Naples. **Page 20.** A philosopher wearing a toga. Mosaic from the second to third centuries A.D. Rheinisches Landesmuseum.

Web Sites

Due to the changing nature of Internet links, PowerKids Press has developed an online list of Web sites related to the subject of this book. This site is updated regularly. Please use this link to access the list:

www.powerkidslinks.com/psaciv/homerom/